Contents

KW-220-920

Communication

An engineer adjusts a dish aerial on a modern communication tower.

Communication is an essential part of our lives. As young children at school, we learn to communicate in a variety of ways. As adults, we possibly spend more time communicating than doing anything else. Recent advancements in science and technology have greatly increased our ability to communicate quickly and over immense distances. When astronauts fly through space or walk on the Moon, we are able to watch them live on television. Pictures of planets, taken by spacecraft, have been sent millions of kilometres through space to Earth. The invention of the microchip has enabled us to link computers and telecommunications systems to send information around the world with great speed. We are in a new age of information technology where words, numbers, sounds and images can be dealt with electronically. As the amount of information being sent around the world increases, new communication technologies continue to be developed.

The worldwide communciation networks we have today use computers, satellites and optical fibres. These modern communication systems have been developed over the years, based on the work of those who invented signalling machines, telephone and telegraph communications. This book discusses early and more

Many young children now use microcomputers as part of their everyday school activities.

modern communication technologies as well as the latest forms of telecommunications, including new communications systems in the office and the home, satellites and optical fibres. There are practical instructions for things to do that relate to the information in the text. The final chapter looks at possible communication systems of the future.

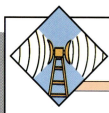

Nature and communication

There are many different ways in which animal species communicate. Dolphins are able to produce squeaks, clicks and grunts. Some scientists believe that dolphins, who have larger brains than humans, have a sophisticated language to communicate with each other. At the beginning of the breeding season the male humpback whales sing a complicated song. By the end of the breeding season the whales have changed the song completely. No one knows why the humpback whales sing. Some scientists believe that one day we will learn how to communicate with these amazing creatures.

Chimpanzees and gorillas are unable to speak like people, but they can make a wide variety of sounds.

These chimpanzees communicate with sound and facial expressions.

Some apes in captivity have been taught to communicate with humans using a simple sign language.

Many animals transmit (send out) warning signals. These are received (picked up) by other animals. For example, a bird's call may warn other birds of the danger from a nearby cat.

Animals use colour signals a great deal. For example, when a peacock displays his beautiful tail to a peahen, he is trying to attract her to mate with him. An Australian lizard called the blue-tongued skink sticks out its bright blue tongue to scare away an enemy.

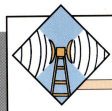

Make a nature scrapbook

1. Visit a library and look at books that will tell you more about communication in the world of nature. Make notes and drawings of interesting points you have learned about nature and communication, and put them in a scrapbook.

Look at any nature magazines you may have at home. If it is possible, cut out pictures to add to your scrapbook.

2. Observe the plants and animals in your garden or in the countryside. Make drawings and take notes of any examples of communication for your scrapbook.

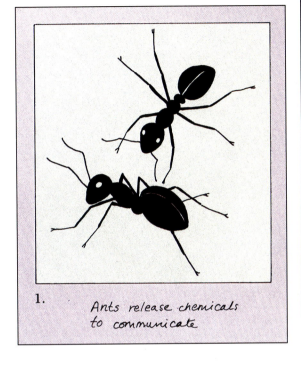

1. *Ants release chemicals to communicate*

2. *Bees dance to communicate direction of food*

There are many ways to organize your scrapbook. You may want to study a particular animal, such as a squirrel, and show the different ways in which it communicates. For example, how does it try to frighten its enemies, attract a mate, or warn other squirrels of danger nearby? You could find pictures of each type of communication to put in your scrapbook. Or you may want to study a particular form of communicating, for example, smell. You could look for different examples of how plants and animals use smell to communicate. Can you think of other ways to organize your nature scrapbook?

Simple communication

One simple method of communicating over a distance is to use a mirror to reflect sunlight. You can do this by moving a mirror to flash spots of sunlight on to a wall. Signalling devices called heliographs were developed to reflect sunlight and communicate messages. Can you think of a drawback to using this method of communication? Another development was to use artificial light, from an electric bulb, and to focus this on to a mirror. Portable signalling lamps were designed from this idea and used on board ships.

Semaphore is a signalling method that uses two flags and a special code. The flags are held in different positions for each letter of the alphabet. Semaphore machines have been built to use this code and send messages over distances. Two hundred years ago a line of semaphore stations, each using large moving wooden arms, was set up in France. Later, many semaphore towers also using movable arms were built in Britain. This method of signalling was adapted for use on railway tracks.

These 19th-century riflemen are using semaphore to send a message.

Design a message machine

You need:

Wood
Mirrors
Elastic bands
3.5 volt bulbs
Bulb-holders
Wood glue
Lengths of wire

4.5 volt batteries
Hacksaw
Bench-hook
Sticky tape
Wire
Plus any other materials you need and can easily obtain

1. Look through this book for ideas. See page 29 on how to build a wood structure. Visit your library to get more ideas. Look carefully at any pictures you find of message machines.

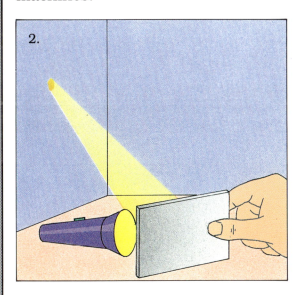

2. Make some sketches of your ideas. Decide which one of your sketches you will be able to make into a working message machine. Make an accurate drawing of the message machine you plan to build.

3. Using the materials you have collected and your drawing, make a message machine. Use your machine to send a message from one side of your classroom to another. Does it work? If not, what changes can be made to make it work?

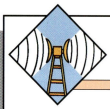

Electricity and magnetism

Communication over very long distances became possible when scientists began to make some important discoveries about electricity and magnetism. An Italian, Alessandro Volta, invented the first electric battery in 1800. Volta used a series of silver and zinc disks in a salt solution to produce an electric current. In 1819 Hans Oersted, in Denmark, found that a wire carrying an electric current could move a magnetic compass needle. This led to the invention of the electromagnet by William Sturgeon, who used electricity to create magentism.

You can make an electromagnet by winding a long length of covered wire around a large iron nail. Connect both ends of the wire to the terminals of a battery, as shown. The electricity flowing through the coil of wire will magnetize the nail. Place the nail next to a pile of paperclips. What happens?

In 1838 Samuel Morse, an American, devised a code to send messages over great distances using an electric circuit. Morse Code uses long (dashes) and short (dots) electrical pulses for different letters of the alphabet.

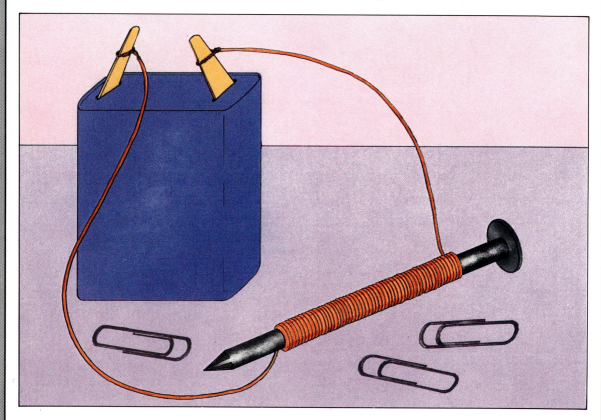

Make a signalling system

You need:
A 4.5 volt battery
Screwdriver
A length of wire
2 pieces of wood
2 3.5 volt bulbs

Glue
2 bulb holders
4 drawing pins
2 paperclips

1. Make a signalling board. Screw a bulb into a bulb-holder. Glue the bulb-holder to a piece of wood. Push two drawing pins into the wood. Position a paperclip on one drawing pin to make a switch, as shown. Connect a short length of wire from one drawing pin to one side of the bulb-holder. Make a second signal board in the same way.

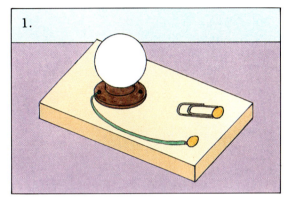

2. Use long lengths of wire to connect the two signal boards to the battery, as shown.

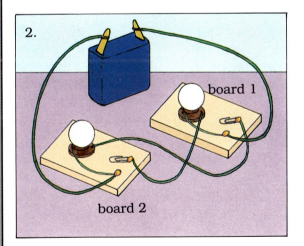

3. When you move the paperclip switch to one side on signal board 1, the bulb on board 2 will light up. Press the switch on board 2 to light the bulb on board 1. Use this system to signal to a friend sitting in another room. Try to use Morse Code.

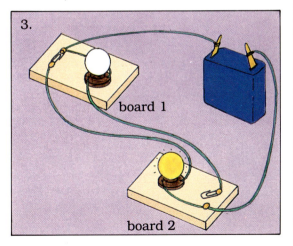

Warning: Do not use mains electricity. It is dangerous.

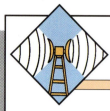

Messages all around us

A traffic sign on a motorway in Germany warns drivers of possible danger.

All around us there are messages giving us information about our world. Many of these messages are communicated to us without using words. Advertisements, for example, often use pictures and images instead of words to encourage us to buy a particular product. Almost everywhere you look – in magazines and newspapers, on television – there are advertisements with beautiful photographs and illustrations that are designed to attract our attention and communicate a message.

Today more and more people travel to other countries, but they do not always understand the language spoken in the country they are visiting. However, communication is possible using signs and symbols that have become internationally recognized. Traffic is controlled with signs and symbols that give directions. Traffic lights use colours to tell drivers and pedestrians when to stop and start. Signs are also used to tell us of possible dangers. What colour comes to mind of when you think of danger?

People sometimes communicate messages without using words. A smile communicates an important message, and so does a frown. Notice the people around you, at your school for instance, and list the ways in which they communicate messages to you without using words.

Make a model traffic light

You need:

3 bulb-holders
3 3.5 volt bulbs
Wire
Paperclips
Glue
2 pieces of wood (40 cm x 15 cm)
Scissors

3 plastic cups
Small screwdriver
4.5 volt battery
4 drawing pins
Red, green and amber tissue paper
Hammer and nails
Wire-stripper

1. Use the hammer and nails to fix the two pieces of wood together. Glue the bulb-holders to the upright piece, as shown. Screw the bulbs into the bulb-holders.

2. Cut six lengths of wire and use the wire-stripper to remove the insulation from each end. Fasten these wires to the bulb-holders, as shown.

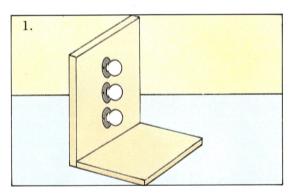

3. Take 3 plastic cups, and cut out the base of each so that they will fit over the bulb-holders. Glue them in place. Stick red, green and amber tissue paper over the lights.

Stick 4 drawing pins on to the baseboard. Place a paperclip over one drawing pin, so that it can be moved, in turn, to the other 3 paperclips. Glue a battery on to the baseboard. Connect wires, as shown, so that the lights can be switched on in turn.

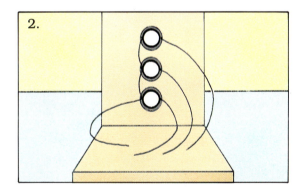

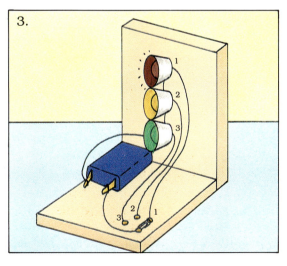

How a telephone works

The telephone was invented by Alexander Graham Bell in 1876. Today, the telephone is a vital part of our lives. We use it to talk to friends and to summon help in emergencies. The telephone makes it possible to communicate instantly with people almost anywhere in the world.

A telephone handset contains two instruments: the mouthpiece, or transmitter, into which you can speak; and the earpiece, or receiver, from which you listen to messages. When you speak into the mouthpiece, the soundwaves from your voice cause a metal disc, called a diaphragm, to vibrate. These vibrations cause carbon granules behind the diaphragm to move. An

Alexander Graham Bell constructed this telephone in 1876.

electric current that flows through these granules is changed by the vibrations. The varying flow of electricity travels along wires to the earpiece of another telephone.

The earpiece contains an electro-magnet and a diaphragm. The changing flow of electricity to the electromagnet causes the diaphragm to vibrate. Sound waves are made, and the listener can hear the speaker's voice.

All telephones are linked to each other through telephone exchanges. Modern telephone exchanges work automatically and can handle millions of calls.

Make a simple telephone

You need:
2 yoghurt pots or polystyrene cups
3 m of thin string
Scissors
Needle

1. Use the needle to make small holes in the base of each yoghurt pot. Cut 3 m of thin string. Thread each end of the string through the yoghurt pots. Inside each pot tie a large knot.

2. Ask a friend to hold one of the yoghurt pots next to his or her ear. Keeping the string tight, talk into your yoghurt pot. Can your friend hear your message?

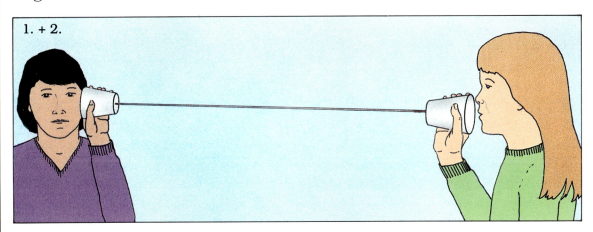

1. + 2.

3. Design and make a simple telephone system so that three people can speak together.

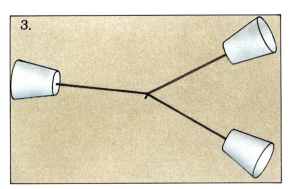

3.

When you speak into the yoghurt pot vibrations from your voice travel along the string. Experiment with your design.

Does the length of string make any difference?

Does thick string work better than thin string?

Does the size of the cups (mouthpiece and receiver) make any difference?

Does the telephone work when the string is slack?

Telegraph messages

The invention of telegraph systems, using electromagnetism, meant that people were able to communicate across great distances of land and sea. Two Englishmen, Charles Wheatstone and William Cooke, saw an early telegraph machine in Germany and then, in 1837, built a device from their own design. Their machine had five needles, each connected to a wire. Electro-magnetism was used to move these needles to point at 20 letters on a grid. Cooke and Wheatstone telegraphs were used in Britain for many years.

By 1845, Samuel Morse, in the USA, was using equipment of his own invention to transmit his dots and dashes code. This system used one instead of five wires and soon began to replace the five-wire system. Before long there were networks of telegraph lines throughout North America and Europe.

In 1855 a British scientist, David Hughes, invented a printing telegraph that turned letters into electrical signals automatically. At the receiving end another machine decoded the signals and printed out the message on a telex teleprinter, which is similar to a typewriter. By the 1860s these messages were being sent along telephone lines rather than telegraph lines.

By 1907 pictures as well as words were being transmitted by a process known as facsimile transmission. It was done by using a photoelectric cell to detect the light and dark areas of a picture that was placed on a rotating drum. These were the first fax machines.

This operator is receiving a message on an early printing telegraph.

Make a telegraph system

You need:
4.5 volt battery
Scissors
Covered wire
3 small pieces of wood
Paperclip

Hammer and nails
5 drawing pins
1 long nail
Thin card

1. Use the battery, a paperclip, two drawing pins, a short length of wire and a piece of wood to make a 'sender board'.

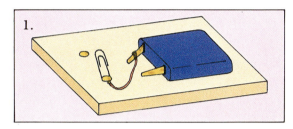

2. To make the 'clicker', first hammer the long nail into a piece of wood. Take a length of wire and wind it around the nail about 60 times. Bare both ends of the wire and fasten them to drawing pins on the board. Fix a small length of wood to the end of the 'clicker' board. This piece of wood needs to be slightly higher than the nailhead. Use a drawing pin to fasten a small strip of card to the top of this wooden piece. Push a paperclip on to the card. The paperclip should be above the nailhead. It should not touch the nail.

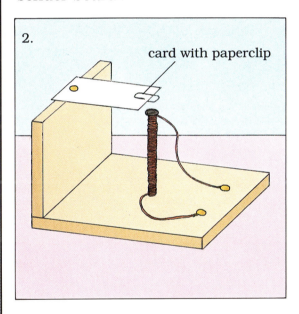

card with paperclip

3. Use two long lengths of wire to connect the sender board to the clicker, as shown. Press the sender board switch on and off. A friend should be able to hear the 'click' as the electromagnet attracts the paperclip. Use your telegraph system to communicate from room to room.

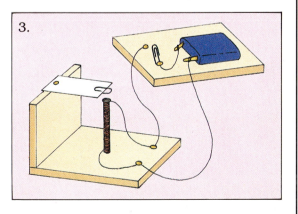

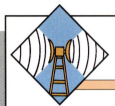

The printed word

In 1438, a German named Johann Gutenberg invented the first mechanical printing press in Europe. This meant that copies of a book could be produced more quickly than ever before. However, books were still quite rare and very expensive. But as printing methods improved, books became much cheaper to produce. Today, books and magazines are mass-produced, and millions of copies of newspapers are printed everyday throughout the world.

Until recently, printing machines called Linotype machines were used to produce lines of type made from lead. These lines of type were arranged, along with special plates for printing pictures, in page-size frames. From these frames, printing plates were made, and these were used to print the pages. Today, many printers use computers (see page 35) for typesetting and printing. A word-processing program is used to input the text to the computer. Any changes can be easily made, and the final version is displayed on the computer screen. When the operator decides everything is correct, the text is printed out by laser on to light-sensitive film. The film is used to make the plate used for printing. This process has made the production of books, magazines and newspapers an even simpler and faster process.

This woman is laying out a page for a newspaper. The finished page will be photographed on to film. The film is then used to make a printing plate. Today, the layout of a newspaper page can be done on a computer screen. The text is printed directly from the computer on to the film from which the plate is made.

Potato printing

You need:
Potatoes
A knife
Pencil and paper
Powder paint

1. Cut a large potato in half. Press the cut end on to a sheet of paper to soak up the moisture.

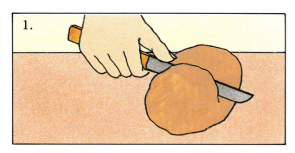

2. Draw two of your initials on a sheet of paper. Make them large enough to fit on the potato ends. Hold the paper against a window pane with the initial facing the glass. Trace the reversed letter shapes on to the other side of the paper.

3. Place the back-to-front letters over the potato ends. Press down hard with the pencil and trace the letters on to the potato.

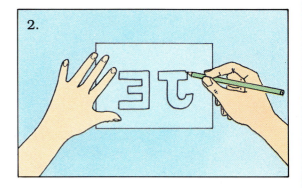

4. Use a knife to cut away the potato to a depth of 0.5 cm around the letters. Brush some thick powder paint on to the letters. Press the letters carefully on to a sheet of paper. They will now be the right way around.

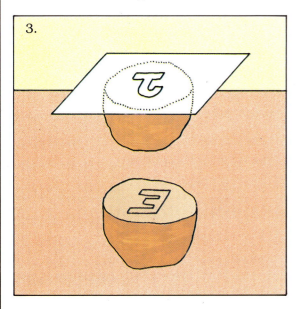

Experiment with different letters so that you can print words.

Photography

From earliest times people have tried to record in pictures the world around them. The invention of photography in the nineteenth century meant that for the first time anyone using a camera could make an accurate image of people and places.

The simplest camera is the pinhole camera. This is a lightproof box with a small hole in one side. Light, which travels in a straight line, passes through the hole and forms an image on the opposite side of the box. The image is upside down.

A more complicated camera has a lens, which is a piece of glass with a curved surface, in place of the hole. The lens is able to produce a sharper and brighter image. The image is then recorded on a film coated with light-sensitive chemicals. The image is later developed (brought out) by treating the film with chemicals. Film can produce black-and-white

Photographers are always eager to take pictures of important events.

or colour pictures depending on the type of chemical coating.

To control the amount of light reaching the film, the aperture (opening) of the lens can be made smaller or larger. A camera also has a shutter, which is a mechanical device that opens and closes to let light in. The faster the shutter speed, the less light is let in. A fast shutter speed is used to take pictures of fast-moving images; the pictures are not blurred because the images are recorded very quickly on to the film. If the shutter speed is very fast, the aperture can be opened wide to provide more light. In modern cameras, electronic devices such as photoelectric cells and microchips automatically adjust the shutter speed and aperture to suit the light condition.

Make a pinhole camera

You need:
A tin can
Hammer and small nail
Greaseproof paper
Sticky tape

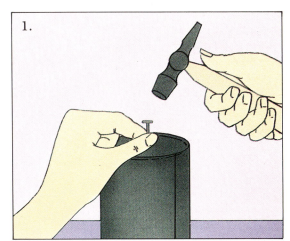

1. Take a clean, empty tin can and make a small hole (no more than 1 mm in diameter) in the base.

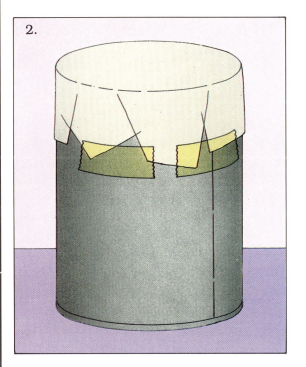

2. Tape some greaseproof paper over the open end of the can.

3. Point your pinhole camera at a bright object. Can you see an upside down image on the greaseproof paper? To make this image clearer, use a tube made from black card.

Try making cameras with different-sized holes. Does this make any difference to the image you can see?

Moving pictures

The films that we see at the cinema are not really moving pictures. They are, in fact, a sequence of still pictures that appear on the screen so quickly that the human eye cannot see the spaces between them. The pictures appear to blend together to make a moving picture.

A cine-camera uses a long strip of film that moves past a shutter and lens. The shutter opens, normally 24 times a second, to let light through the lens and expose a succession of images on to the film. The film is shown on a screen by using a projector. This machine uses powerful lamps to produce a beam of light and project the images on to a screen. The projector also has a shutter mechanism that opens 24 times a second. The result is that the images on screen appear to move as they did in real life.

Sound can also be added to moving pictures. Sound waves are changed into electrical patterns, which are then put along the edge of the film and are known as the sound track. When the film is shown, either a beam of light or an electromagnet changes the electrical patterns of the sound waves back into the original sounds, which are relayed through the cinema loudspeaker system.

This film strip shows four separate pictures that will be seen as a 'moving picture'.

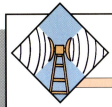

Make a zoetrope

You need:

Thick card	Sticky tape	2 cotton reels
Scissors	A compass	Dowel rod
Thin card	Piece of wood	Wood glue

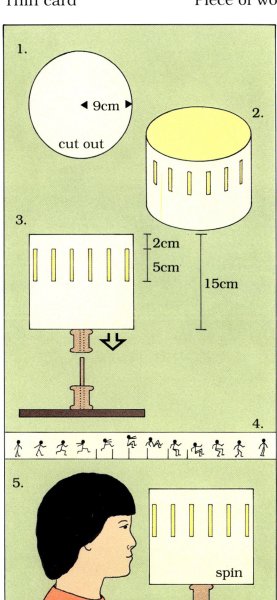

1. Draw a circle of radius 9 cm on thick card. Carefully cut round the circumference. This is to be the base of your zoetrope.

2. Using thin card, cut a rectangle measuring 57 cm x 15 cm. Use a sharp knife to cut 12 slits, each measuring 5 cm x 0.5 cm, as shown. Curve the rectangle of thin card around the thick card circle to form a drum. Use sticky tape to hold them together.

3. Glue a cotton reel to a wood base. Cut a 12-cm length of dowel rod and place it inside the cotton reel. Glue it firmly in place. Glue a second cotton reel in the centre of the base of the cardboard drum. Place the drum on to the dowel rod. Spin the drum. It should revolve freely.

4. Cut a length of thin card measuring 57 cm x 6 cm. Draw twelve pictures on this strip. Each picture should be slightly different to give the impression of movement.

5. Place this picture strip into the drum so that it is under the slits. Spin the drum and look through the slits to see the moving pictures.

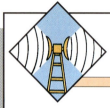

Radio waves

A policeman sending a radio message from a remote area of Australia.

When we communicate using radio waves, the sender and receiver are not connected by wires. At one time this form of communication was known as 'wireless'.

Radio waves are a form of energy that belong to the same group as X-rays and light. They all travel through space or air in the form of electromagnetic waves. The sounds that are made in a broadcasting studio are sent out, in the form of radio waves, from a transmitter aerial. They travel over vast distances to receiver aerials. The radio waves travel in straight lines at the speed of light (nearly 300,000 km per second). Once the radio waves are received, they are converted back to sound waves. Radio receiver aerials may be external (outside) or internal (contained inside the device).

Radio is an important means of communicating. It brings information and entertainment to our homes and cars. Radio messages are sent to ships and aeroplanes. The police, ambulances, taxi-cabs, fire engines and doctors use 'intercom' radios. Can you think of other ways we use radio?

Radio on the move

Many people want to keep in contact as they move around the country by car or train. A new cellular radio system allows users to carry a portable cellphone in their hand or car. These phones operate within small areas, or cells, each of which has its own radio transmitter/receiver. The cell transmitters are linked up to electronic telephone exchanges, so the cellphone user can be connected to the telephone network or to other cellphone users. It is now possible to use a portable phone to make a telephone call to any part of the world.

Some people who move around a great deal in their jobs can be contacted by radio-paging. A radio-pager is a very small radio receiver that can fit into a handbag or pocket. Each radio-pager has a special code number and 'bleeps' when a message is sent out from a radio transmitter. The carrier then knows that he or she needs to telephone a particular number. Some radio-pagers can even display short written messages.

This woman is contacting her office with a cellphone.

Television

Almost all young children love to watch cartoons on television.

Television enables us to see and hear events that are happening many kilometres away. A television camera follows the event to be televised and changes the images into electric signals. The camera uses an electron gun to scan the picture image on a target screen within the camera, one line after another. Each line is changed into a series of electromagnetic pulses. The signals are amplified (made stronger) before being sent to our homes, where television receivers change them back into pictures. The greater the number of lines used in one complete scan on the target screen, the better the quality of the picture produced.

The sound of an event is picked up by microphones, which change the sounds into electric signals. Both the audio (sound) and video (vision) signals are sent out to our homes from tall transmission aerials. Both signals – sound and vision – are carried on continuous electro-magnetic waves. These waves are invisible and travel at the speed of light. Aerials on the roofs of our homes detect these waves. The television receiver converts these signals into sound through a loudspeaker, and into pictures that form on the television screen through a device called a cathode-ray tube. This picture tube contains an electron beam that is focused on a screen and scans it just like the camera tube beam. Special signals are transmitted along with the picture signals to ensure that the camera scans and the picture scans, in the television receiver, are in step. The sound and vision signals coming from an event together form a television channel.

The first television pictures were black and white, but now we are able to see colour pictures. The light entering the lens of a colour television camera is split into red, green and blue components using special mirrors. Each of these colours has its own electron gun so that three separate picture signals are obtained. These signals are combined and sent to aerials on our homes. A colour television receiver separates the three colour signals and sends each one to an electron gun. Three beams of electrons are focused on the screen and scan it at high speed. Near the screen, a plate, called a shadow mask, contains thousands of small holes. Beams from the electron guns move across these holes and cause tiny red, green and blue phosphor dots to glow. In this way, a picture that consists of tiny coloured dots is formed on the screen. Some portable television receivers use a single electron gun in

This television camera is filming a scene from a play.

a more compact design to produce colour pictures.

Some television stations use cables to carry their television broadcasts direct to people's homes. Other television companies are using satellites (see page 30) to beam television signals all over the Earth. Television programme-makers often tape their programmes on videotape machines. These machines, which use special plastic tapes to record pictures and sound in the form of magnetic signals, are now used in many homes.

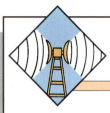

Communication towers

In order to deal with the growing number of telephone calls, television pictures and computer data being sent over great distances, very high communication towers have been built. These towers transmit and receive a special type of radio wave, called a microwave, that has a very short wavelength. Microwaves can be focused into beams, which carry large amounts of information, and sent direct, in a straight line, to a target receiver. The bowl-shaped aerials on each tower receive and then re-transmit the microwave signals. At each tower, the microwaves are electronically amplified before they are re-transmitted.

The transmitter must be pointed directly at the receiver. If anything gets in the path of the microwave beam, there will be interference. Because microwaves travel in straight lines and cannot bend to follow the curvature of the Earth's surface, communication towers must be very tall. A whole network of these towers is needed to beam microwaves all over the country.

Some of these towers are built on top of hills. Look for communication towers when you are in the countryside. Are there any in your area?

Communication towers receive and transmit microwaves. This tower is in the Alps.

A communication tower

You need:

Some lengths of 1 cm x 1 cm wood
Hacksaw
Bench-hook
Ruler, pencil, scissors
Thin card
Paper
P.V.A. glue
Yoghurt pots

1. Use a pencil and ruler to draw horizontal, vertical and diagonal lines on a sheet of thin card. Cut out about 50 triangles.

2. Use the hacksaw and bench-hook to cut 4 90-cm and 12 20-cm lengths of wood. Ask an adult to supervise you.

3. Use the card triangles and P.V.A. to fix the wood together as shown. Each corner joint is made by applying some P.V.A. to a card triangle and positioning it over the corner, as shown. Let the corner joints dry. Card triangles should be fixed to both sides of each corner joint.

Cut lengths of wood to fit diagonally, to give strength to the structure as shown.

Use thin card or yoghurt pots to make some microwave dish aerials. Fix these to the wooden tower.

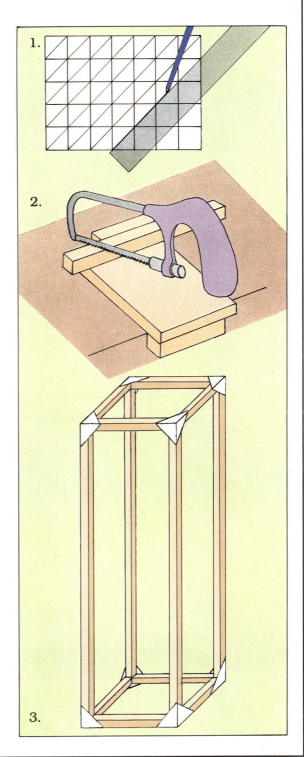

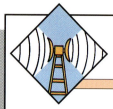

Communications satellites

Communications satellites are launched into space and orbit the Earth. They allow us to watch live television pictures of events happening on the other side of the world. They relay telephone calls, computer data and other information. *Telstar*, the first communications satellite to transmit live television pictures between the USA and Britain, was launched into orbit in 1962. *Telstar* could also carry up to sixty telephone conversations. In 1965, the American communications satellite *Intelsat I* became the first commercial satellite to provide a constant link between North America and Europe. Since then there have been great advancements in satellite communications, and many more satellites have been sent into orbit. Modern communications satellites can carry two television channels and up to 2,000 telephone conversations.

Communications satellites go into a very high orbit above the Earth's surface, right around the Equator. In this orbit, the satellites travel at the same speed as the Earth rotates, so they appear to hover directly above one place on the Earth's surface. This kind of orbit is called a geostationary orbit.

A transmitter station on the Earth sends microwaves in the form of a narrow beam to a satellite in space. The satellite receives the message,

A communications satellite orbiting the Earth. Communications satellites transmit and receive messages to and from the Earth.

which has travelled thousands of kilometres and is quite weak, and strengthens the signals before beaming them back to a receiver dish in another part of the Earth. Only three satellites, spaced around the globe in geostationary orbit, are needed to transmit and receive messages to and from any part of the Earth's surface.

Make a model satellite

You need:

Some lengths of 1 cm x 1 cm wood
Large tin can
Washing-up liquid bottle
Hacksaw
Bench-hook
Thin and thick card
Yoghurt pots
P.V.A. glue
Dowel rod
Paint and brushes

1. Use the wood structures method (see page 29) to make the framework for a ground station.

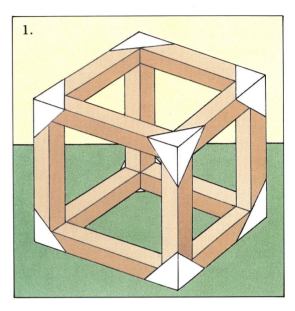

2. Use thick card to make a dish-shaped aerial. Fix this aerial to the framework using the dowel rod. Use card and paint to make your model more realistic.

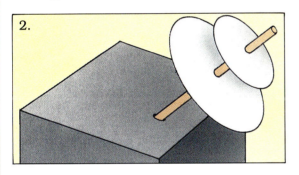

3. Look at the photograph of a satellite. Design and make a model satellite to hang in your classroom. What materials will you use? Real satellites are of different shapes. They do not need to be streamlined since there is no air in space. Satellites use solar cells to give power. Sunlight falls on these solar cells and they produce electricity. How could you fix an electric circuit (see page 11) on your model satellite?

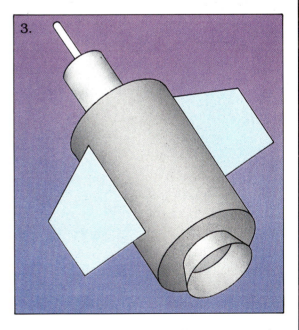

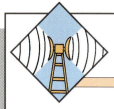

Cables under the sea

During the past 140 years, a network of communication cables have been laid under the seas of the world. The first telegraph cable to join Britain and the USA, across the Atlantic, was laid in 1866. By the early 1900s, undersea telegraph cables connected all the continents.

The first undersea cables were ordinary telegraph cables protected and strengthened with galvanized iron wires. The development of more efficient cables, known as co-axial cables, led to the first transatlantic telephone service coming into use in 1956. This service consisted of two cables (one for each direction of transmission) with amplifiers, or repeaters, installed at intervals along the cables to boost the signals. Thirty-six two-way telephone circuits were provided by this cable.

Cable-laying ships are used to carry and lay the cables, which may be several hundred kilometres long. Steel 'armour' may protect the aluminium or copper conductors. Sometimes to avoid damage, the cables are buried under the sea-bed. A remote-controlled vehicle, with caterpillar tracks and controlled from a cable-ship, is often used to do this job. In 1988 the first trans-atlantic optical fibre cable (see page 40) was laid. It is able to carry 40,000 simultaneous telephone calls.

The first cable was laid across the Atlantic in 1866.

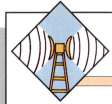

Digital transmission

Most telephone exchanges now use digital transmission.

The early telegraph systems transmitted their signals using a series of on/off electrical pulses. This is called a digital system. The first telephones worked by taking the sound waves and changing them into continuous electrical waves for transmission down cables. At the receiver end, the electrical waves were changed back into sound waves. This is described as an analogue system because the signal exactly reproduces the sound being made. It worked well over short distances, but when longer cables were used, the transmitted signal began to fade. One solution is to turn speech into a series of electrical pulses at the transmitter. At the receiver they are turned back into speech. This digital method (using the binary digits zero and one) of sending signals became possible when transistors, which use digital information, were invented.

Since the development of the microchip, digital transmission is widely used. Telephone exchanges all over the world are being changed to cope with digital transmission. It is an essential part of the telecommunications revolution.

The microchip revolution

Early radios and televisions used valves to amplify an electric current and as electronic switches. Valves were also used in the first computers. But valves are quite large and often unreliable, and they become very hot with use. In 1947 in the USA, three scientists, named John Bardeen, Walter Brattain and William Shockley, invented a new electronic device called a transistor. It could do the same job as a valve but was more reliable and did not need to warm up as a valve did. The transistor also has the great advantage of being very small. Soon portable transistor radios became available. Transistors were also replacing valves in computers, which as a result were becoming much smaller.

By the 1960s, scientists developed a new way of making a number of transistors on one side of a flat material called silicon. This method led to the development of integrated circuits, also known as silicon chips or microchips. Today, a single microchip may contain thousands of transistors. The chip itself may be so small that it could pass through the eye of a needle. Each silicon chip, complete with integrated circuit, is fitted into a plastic case for easy handling.

The silicon chip, or microchip, revolutionized communications. This new technology made it possible to

Microchips are so small that they can go through the eye of a threaded needle.

achieve greater speed and efficiency in communication and even further reductions in the size of communication equipment.

Computers

Inside the busy computer room of a large organization.

Computers handle information almost instantly. They can do routine work that would take a person a great deal of time and effort. The first generation of computers were built more than forty years ago using thousands of valves. Today, special microchips, known as microprocessors, are used to build computers and microcomputers, which are much smaller and a great deal more powerful. Data is entered into the computer using a keyboard and is stored on magnetic tape or special disks. A vast amount of information can be stored on these disks, which take up far less space than conventional files. New optical disks, using lasers to store and read the data, are being developed. A complete dictionary can be stored on one optical disk.

A computer is fed a series of special instructions called a program, which tells the machine how to carry out a particular task. Computer programs are written in a special computer language. Data can be read from a television or visual display screen (VDU), and a permanent printout is obtained by using a printer. Computers are now used in many different ways, in offices, homes and schools.

Office communications

Many offices now have equipment that has been developed by using microchips and modern communication systems. Files containing information on, for example, customers and staff can be stored using computers. Written messages that need to be delivered quickly can be sent by telex or teleprinter. Modern telex machines are computer controlled. These machines are able to store a message and then transmit it, at a required time, over any of the 2 million lines throughout the world.

Teletex is a new electronic mail service that is thirty times faster than telex. The equipment needed is a special teletex terminal or simply an electronic typewriter or computer fitted with a teletex adaptor. A person can prepare a letter on the teletex terminal and then send it over the network to many different destinations. There is no need for stamps, envelopes or posting, and the letter will arrive at its destination almost instantaneously. Both the telex and teletex mail services include special coded messages to identify the sender and receiver.

Facsimile, or fax, is a system for sending diagrams, pictures or documents over the telephone network. A modern fax machine changes the images on a diagram into electrical pulses. These pulses travel through the telephone system to a receiver fax machine. The pulses are then used to produce a copy of the original diagram on a printer. The photographs used in newspapers have often been faxed from around the world, via undersea cables or beamed via satellites.

In 1979, the British Post Office launched the first viewdata system, known as Prestel. Information, which has been supplied by banks, stores, newspapers and government bodies, is stored on a central computer, or database. A user can gain access to the database via the telephone system.

When people from one office need to speak to others in an office some distance away, they can use either teleconferencing or videoconferencing. This eliminates the need to travel great distances for meetings and thus saves time and money. When people have a teleconference, they cannot see each other, but they can conduct their meeting using the telephone. A special electronic writing board can be used to illustrate diagrams and charts to all the people at the meeting. Videoconferencing uses television cameras and monitors so that the people can see each other. The meeting can be conducted as if they were sitting across a table.

Microcomputers are an important feature in many modern offices.

At home and at school

Communication systems within homes are already changing at a rapid pace. There are a whole range of modern telephone services that can do more than just receive and make calls. If you go to a neighbour's home you can transfer all in-coming calls to your neighbour's telephone number. Telephone numbers that you use frequently can be stored in the telephone's memory. To call one of these numbers you use a short code rather than the full telephone number.

It is even possible to have a home telephone that does not need a long telephone cable. These telephones are known as 'cordless phones'. An adaptor is fitted to your conventional telephone, and this sends radio waves to your cordless phone. Your conversation is relayed back and forth to the adaptor by these waves.

More and more people have micro-computers at home for their private use. There are a great number of computer games available and these have become a popular form of home entertainment. Computers are also used to keep track of household accounts and to store other information.

Most schools now have computers. They are used for word-processing, for storing information and for controlling simple devices, such as the model traffic lights described on page 13.

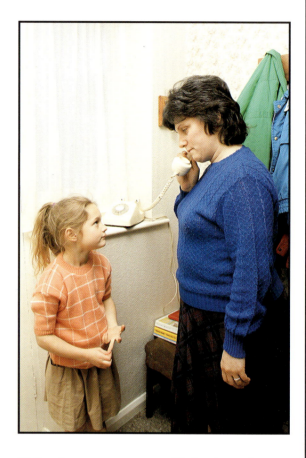

Telephones are an efficient and convenient way of keeping in touch with friends, whether they live nearby or thousands of kilometres away.

Some television sets are equipped with viewdata systems. Their users have access to a vast range of information, including sports results and weather conditions, at the touch of a button. It is also possible to use the telephone and television set (or computer monitor) at home to provide an exciting new

Small but very sophisticated microcomputers can be found in many homes, and they have become a popular form of home entertainment.

method of communication. The viewer uses a keyboard to question a central computer, which has over 350,000 pages of information available. These pages provide very up-to-date information on business and government data, travel timetables and leisure pursuits. In the future this service will probably be linked up to banks so that people can check their accounts and pay bills whilst sitting at home. This system could also be used to do the weekly shopping. The central computer would be linked to the supermarket computer so that prices could be checked and orders placed. If you know someone with this sort of communication system, ask them to show you how it works.

Optical fibres

Optical fibres are at the centre of a new era in telecommunications.

Optical fibres are a recent development in the field of communications. An optical fibre is made of the purest glass and is no thicker than a human hair. A single cable containing several optical fibres can carry many thousands of telephone conversations at the same time. The messages are sent along each fibre using pulses of light rather than electricity. The signal that is to be transmitted is used to control a light source, such as a laser, and the light from this is fed into the fibre. The fibre is specially made so that light entering at one end travels to the other. The sides of the fibre reflect the light inwards, so that none escapes.

Optical fibre cables are now replacing conventional copper cables. They are cheaper, easier to handle and enable us to have interference-free telephone calls. It is predicted that by the end of this century all of Europe and the USA will use optical fibre cable networks. Computer data, television pictures and telephone messages will all be sent using light pulses.

Using a light pipe

You need:
Some kitchen foil
A pencil
Sticky tape
Screw driver
Pieces of wood
3.5 volt bulb
4.5 volt battery
Wire
Paperclips
Fibre optic material (from supplier on page 46)

2. Glue two pieces of wood together. Glue a bulb-holder to the vertical piece of wood. Screw in a bulb and connect it to a battery, as shown.

1. Wrap the kitchen foil, shiny side on the inside, carefully around the pencil. Fix it in place with sticky tape. Slide the pencil out so that you are left with a pipe of foil.

3. Place your foil pipe in front of the bulb. Notice how light from the bulb can travel down the pipe on to a piece of card.

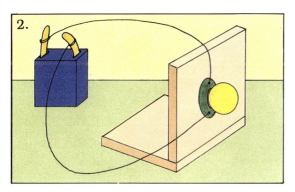

4. Take a length of fibre optic material and coil it as shown. Place one end next to the light bulb. Look at the other end. It is lit up because light from the bulb has travelled down the cable. What other uses can you think of for this material?

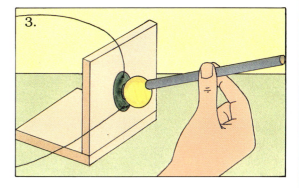

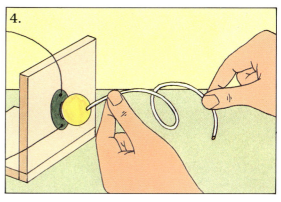

The future

It is extremely difficult to make predictions because changes are happening very quickly in communication technology. Already pocket-phones are being used. These small devices can make outgoing calls when they are within 200 m of a base station. This base station receives the signal from the pocket-phone and links it up to the conventional telephone network. Pocket-phones are much cheaper than cellular telephones, but they cannot, at present, be used to receive calls. Maybe in the very near future we will have our own portable communications terminal. We will be able to carry it in our pockets and use it in the street, in our cars and even in trains or on aeroplanes.

New developments in transmitting moving colour pictures and sound on telephone lines could lead to videophones. You could be able to see the person at the other end as well as hear them. Special desk-top videoconferencing units are being designed for use by business people. Each unit will include a phone and television screen and two video cameras. One camera is used to film the user. The other camera can film paperwork or any object the user wishes to show. These desk-top units will be suitable for use all over the world.

Many people spend their working lives moving from place to place. Salespeople are now using portable telephones while they travel in their cars. More people will make use of portable or laptop computers to store information and for word-processing. It is already possible to write a report using a word-processor or a portable computer, and then to transmit this report through the telephone system using a portable car-phone. It may well be that in the future more and more people will have their cars fitted out as mobile offices.

Huge bowl-shaped aerials receive signals from deep into space.

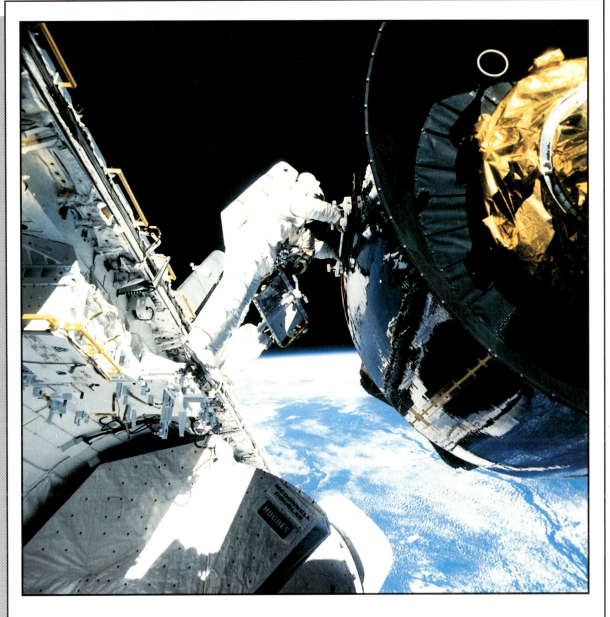

Astronauts are able to repair communications satellites in space.

On the other hand it is predicted that many people will not need to travel to work. They will not need to waste time in traffic jams or on trains. Instead they will work from home using computers and have access to all the information they need through data-banks and the telecommunications network. The computers themselves will also change. Developments in electronics will make them even more powerful and easier to use.

At school you are now using computers for word-processing and for storing and having access to data. How do you think computers will change school life in the future?

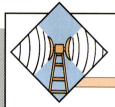

Glossary

Amplifier An electronic device, such as a transistor or a valve, that increases the strength of an electrical signal.

Cathode-ray tube An electronic device in which a beam of electrons (cathode rays) are made to strike a fluorescent screen, which glows as a result.

Cine-camera A motion picture camera.

Computer An electronic machine that can perform a variety of calculations and act as a memory store. These calculations are controlled by a series of instructions, known as a program, that are fed into the machine.

Data-bank A store of data on a disk or tape.

Electric current The flow of 'free' electrons through a conductor.

Electrical pulse A short burst of electric current.

Electromagnet A temporary magnet formed by winding a coil of wire around a piece of iron. An electrical current flowing in the wire causes the iron to become magnetized, and a varying electrical current produces a corresponding variation in the magnetic field.

Electromagnetic waves Invisible waves, composed of vibrating electrical and magnetic fields, that travel at the speed of light. They include X-rays, ultra-violet rays, light, infra-red rays, microwaves and radio waves.

Electronics Concerned with the accurately controlled flow of electric currents using special devices such as transistors.

Electrons Minute, negatively-charged particles that move around the nucleus of an atom.

Integrated circuit A complicated electrical circuit formed on a piece of silicon.

Laser A device for producing a narrow beam of bright light. The name is short for Light Amplification by Stimulated Emission of Radiation.

Microchip A tiny bit of silicon on which electronic circuits are printed.

Microcomputer A small computer that can be carried.

Phosphor A substance that emits light when it is bombarded with electrons.

Photoelectric cell A device in which light energy is converted into electrical energy.

Radio The use of electromagnetic waves to transmit electrical signals without wires.

Satellite A spacecraft that moves around, or orbits, a planet or star.

Telecommunications The branch of technology that deals with communication over long distances, by cable, telegraph, telephone or broadcasting.

Telegraph A method of communication that involves sending coded electrical signals by wire or radio.

Teletex A form of telegraph used for sending text from one word processor to another.

Television A system for sending and receiving pictures using radio waves.

Telex A form of telegraph used for sending and receiving text. Letters typed by the sender are automatically encoded and transmitted by the sender's machine. On arrival at the receiver's machine, they are decoded and printed out.

Transmitter A machine for sending out radio pulses.

Transistor An electronic device that controls pulses of electricity by acting as a switch.

Word processor A computer or computer program designed specially for producing printed text.

Notes for parents and teachers

This book will be useful to teachers in implementing the National Curriculum at Key Stages 1, 2 and 3. The information and activities relate to the following:

Technology attainment targets 1, 2, 3, 4 and 5.
Science attainment targets 1, 2, 3, 5, 6, 9, 10, 11, 12, 13, 14, 15 and 16.

Communications can also be developed as a cross-curricular topic that includes National Curriculum English and Mathematics.

There are many activities in this book that will require the help of a teacher or parent. Parents will also find it helpful to consult the section on places to visit during weekends and school holidays.

Further information

Books to read

Bowen-Davies, W., *The How and Why Wonder Book of Communications* (Transworld, 1973)

Byrne, T. and Gregory, T., *Inside Story – Television* (Wayland, 1989)

Carey, D., *How it Works – the Telephone* (Ladybird, 1978)

Catherall, E., *Electric Power* (Wayland, 1981)

De Bono, E. (ed), *Eureka! An Illustrated History of Inventions* (Thames and Hudson, 1979)

Dixon, M., *Batteries, Bulbs and Circuits* (Edward Arnold, 1982)

Dixon, M., *Magnets and Electromagnets* (Edward Arnold, 1982)

Irvine, M., *TV and Video* (Franklin Watts, 1983)

Kurth, H., *Computers* (World's Work Ltd, 1982)

Macaulay, D. and Ardley, N., *The Way Things Work* (Dorling, Kindersley, 1988)

Mayall, W.H., *The Challenge of the Chip* (HMSO, 1980)

Purnell's Encyclopaedia of Inventions (Purnell, 1976)

Slater, D., *Information Technology* (Franklin Watts/Aladdin Books, 1986)

Storris, G., *The Telecommunications Revolution* (Wayland, 1985)

Sturridge, M., *Micro-Computers* (Kingfisher Books Ltd, 1983)

Wicks, K., *Television* (Macdonald Educational, 1975)

Organizations to contact

British Telecom
Education Service
British Telecom Centre
Floor B4
81 Newgate Street
London
EC1A 7AJ

Kodak Ltd
P O Box 66
Station Road
Hemel Hempstead
HP1 1JU

Technology Teaching Systems
Penmore House
Hasland Road
Hasland
Chesterfield
S41 OSJ
(Supplier of fibre optic material)

Understanding Electricity
The Electricity Council
30 Millbank
London
SW1P 4RD

Places to visit

British Telecom Museum
35 Speedwell Street
Oxford
OX1 1RM

British Telecom Museum
Telephone Exchange
St Andrews Street
Norwich

The Engineerium
Nevill Road
Hove
East Sussex

Goonhilly Satellite Earth Station
Goonhilly Down
Helston
Cornwall
TR12 6LQ

Greater Manchester Museum
  of Science and Industry
Liverpool Road
Manchester
M3 4JP

The Milne Electricity Museum
Tonbridge
Kent

Royal Museum of Scotland
Chambers Street
Edinburgh
EH1 1JF

Science Museum
Exhibition Road
South Kensington
London

Telecom Technology Showcase
135 Queen Victoria Street
London
EC4V 4AT

Young Designers Centre
Haymarket
London
SW1

You could also visit local telephone exchanges. School parties are welcome by prior arrangement. Look in your telephone directory for the address.

Picture acknowledgements

The publishers would like to thank the following for supplying pictures British Telecom (Telefocus) cover, 4, 33, 41; Hulton Picture Library 32; Jim Finler 22; Oxford Scientific Films 6; Research House 43; Ann Ronan 8, 16; Science Photo Library 34; Topham 9; Wayland Picture Library 18, 24, 27, 37; Zefa 5, 12, 14, 25, 26, 28, 30, 35, 38, 39, 40.

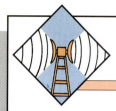

Index